.75

D1122986

ROSEMARY

ROSEMARY

A Book of Recipes

INTRODUCTION BY KATE WHITEMAN

LORENZ BOOKS
NEW YORK • LONDON • SYDNEY • BATH

First published by Lorenz Books in 1997

Lorenz Books is an imprint of
Anness Publishing Inc.
27 West 20th Street
New York, NY 10011

© 1997 Anness Publishing Limited

ISBN 1 85967 489 5

Publisher Joanna Lorenz
Senior Cookery Editor Linda Fraser
Project Editor Anne Hildyard
Designer Bill Mason
Illustrations Anna Koska

Photographers Karl Adamson, Edward Allwright, James Duncan, John Freeman,
Michelle Garrett and Patrick McLeavey
Recipes Catherine Atkinson, Jacqueline Clark, Joanna Farrow, Christine France,
Shirley Gill, Christine Ingram, Maggie Pannell, Liz Trigg and Steven Wheeler
Food for photography Jacqueline Clark, Joanna Farrow, Katherine Hawins
and Jane Stevenson
Stylists Madeleine Brehaut, Hilary Guy, Blake Minton and Kirsty Rawlings
Jacket photography Janine Hosegood

Printed and bound in China

For all recipes, quantities are given in standard cups and spoons, or, where
applicable, in imperial measures.

1 3 5 7 9 10 8 6 4 2

Contents

Introduction 6

Fish and Seafood 12

Meat Dishes 18

Poultry Dishes 32

Vegetable Dishes and Breads 42

Vinegars, Preserves, and Drinks 56

Index 64

$\mathcal{I}$NTRODUCTION

An intensely aromatic shrub native to Mediterranean countries, rosemary grows happily in sandy, rocky places with scanty soil. It takes its name from the Latin *Rosmarinus*, rose of the sea, and can often be found growing on the sides of cliffs or near the shore. Rosemary is also widely cultivated in gardens, where it is valued for its pleasant aroma, culinary and medicinal uses, and for the protection it gives against insect pests.

There are countless picturesque legends associated with rosemary and the belief in its mystic powers persisted for centuries. It was the symbol of friendship and the custom was for friends of a dead person to throw sprays of rosemary "for remembrance" into the grave. Sprays were also strewn before a bride.

Rosemary has always been a favorite with gypsies. They used to peddle a preparation made from flowering rosemary sprigs, known as Queen of Hungary's Water. It was much valued by women as a cure-all and beauty tonic. Gypsies also kept a sprig in their vans to protect against evil forces and tucked it under a child's pillow to prevent nightmares. The Arabs used dried powdered rosemary as an antiseptic for the umbilical cord of new-born babies. The Spanish also believed in rosemary's antiseptic powers; they pounded it with salt to make a paste which they then applied to wounds.

The small, needle-like leaves are dark green, tough, and very aromatic. Their volatile oils stimulate the secretion of digestive juices and so arouse the appetite. Whole leaves are too spiky for comfort so they need to be very finely chopped or, if left on a sprig, removed before serving. The blue-mauve flowers are said to have originally been white, but there is a legend that the Virgin Mary rested beside a rosemary bush on her flight into Egypt and threw her robe over it; the flowers turned blue in her honor. They look pretty scattered over strawberries or poached pears.

Rosemary combines well with meat, particularly fatty varieties, such as lamb and pork. It is also good mixed with lemon zest in fish dishes, stuffings, and tomato-based sauces. A small sprig adds a subtle flavor to milk used for desserts and to syrups for fruit salads.

This book begins with advice on how to grow, prepare and store rosemary. The first chapter shows how rosemary adds pungency to fish and seafood dishes. The chapters on meat and poultry will have you smacking your lips in anticipation. We go on to show how rosemary's powerful presence adds depth to vegetarian and vegetable dishes, breads, pasta, and pizza. The final chapter offers a delightful and surprising selection of vinegars, preserves, and drinks.

TYPES OF ROSEMARY

STANDARD BUSH

Rosemary bushes (*Rosmarinus officinalis*) tend to grow quite vigorously, quickly reaching a height of 5 feet when planted in an open border. However, they also flourish in containers, a method of cultivation that provides greater control, and are well suited to planting in a raised bed. 'Tuscan Blue' and 'Majorca Pink' are ideal varieties for the smaller garden or patio, as they have neat growth, bright, ornamental flowers, and are excellent for all purposes, including cooking. The variety known as var. *albiflorus* has white flowers. There are also some varieties with gold or silver stripes on the leaves, but these are less hardy than common green rosemary. These tend to be grown for ornamental rather than culinary purposes.

'SILVER SPIRES'

An old variety with mid-blue flowers and fine silvery leaves, this is more usually grown for its appearance rather than for culinary or medicinal use.

'MISS JESSOPP'S UPRIGHT'

Also known as 'Fastigiatus,' this is a tall, hardy upright variety with lighter green leaves than normal and pale blue flowers.

PROSTRATE

The prostrate version (*Rosmarinus officinalis* 'Prostratus') has fine leaves and bright blue flowers. Like other trailing varieties, it is tender and needs heat in winter in order to survive. It grows well in rock gardens.

SEMI-PROSTRATE

While more vigorous in habit than prostrate varieties, semi-prostrate rosemary tends to be less rampant than standard bushes. The best-known semi-prostrate variety is 'Severn Sea.'

DRIED ROSEMARY

Rosemary is one of the few herbs whose leaves keep their flavor well when they have been dried. Store them in an airtight, dark glass jar away from heat and light. However, as all varieties of rosemary are evergreen, the fresh leaves are available all year.

WHOLE STEMS

Woody rosemary stems create a wonderful aroma when burned on the barbecue or on an open fire. They are traditionally burned when Easter lamb is spit-roasted after the Lenten fast in eastern Orthodox countries.

Powdered dried
rosemary

Woody rosemary stem

Chopped dried
rosemary

Prostrate

'Silver Spires'

'Miss Jessopp's Upright'

Rosemary

$\mathscr{B}$ASIC $\mathscr{T}$ECHNIQUES

—— PREPARING ROSEMARY ——

Rub your fingers down the woody stem two or three times to strip off all the leaves.

To chop the leaves very finely, use a very sharp knife with a curved blade or a mezzaluna.

Tender leaves from the tip of a young rosemary shoot can simply be snipped off with scissors.

COOK'S TIPS

• *Rosemary with poultry* When broiling chicken, tuck small sprigs of rosemary under the skin.

• *Rosemary oil* Put a large sprig of rosemary in a bottle of olive oil and leave for two weeks before using to allow the flavor to develop.

• *Rosemary stuffing* A tablespoon of finely chopped rosemary combined with breadcrumbs, lemon rind, egg, and

seasoning makes a delicious stuffing for poultry or breast of lamb.

• *Rosemary with olives* Store black olives in a screw-top container with plenty of chopped rosemary. Add enough olive oil to cover. The olives will keep for several weeks.

• *Rosemary sugar* Put a sprig of rosemary in a jar of sugar and use in baking and desserts.

RECIPE IDEAS

Grated zucchini with rosemary Put 3–4 grated zucchini in a pan with salt, pepper, finely chopped rosemary, and a knob of butter. Cover and cook over medium heat for 5 minutes, shaking the pan occasionally. Stir in cream and heat through.

Rosemary and roasted beet Roast peeled beet with olive oil, chili flakes, and a few sprigs of tender, young rosemary.

Plum compote with rosemary For a delicious compote, cook halved plums in a sugar syrup flavored with orange peel and a sprig of rosemary.

Rosemary sauce Dice 1 onion and 1 apple and fry in 2 tbsp butter. Stir 1 tbsp cornstarch into 1¼ cups light stock, add to the pan, stir in 5 tbsp tomato paste and bring to a boil. Sieve and reheat with sugar and finely chopped rosemary.

ROSEMARY SHORTBREAD
Serves 4

Pound 2 tbsp finely chopped rosemary with ¼ cup superfine sugar. Sift 1 cup all-purpose flour and ½ cup rice flour into a bowl. Mix in the rosemary sugar and ½ tsp vanilla extract. Rub in ½ cup butter and knead the mixture into a ball. Place on a board sprinkled with rice flour and press into an 8in diameter round. Place on a greased cookie sheet and prick all over the surface with a fork. Pinch the edges with your fingers. Bake in a preheated oven at 350°F for 20–30 minutes until pale golden in color. Mark into eight segments and leave to cool completely on the cookie sheet.

Fish and Seafood

Combined with other robust ingredients, such as wine and tomatoes, rosemary adds richness to sauces and marinades for Mediterranean-style fish and seafood dishes.

SALMON WITH ROSEMARY MARINADE

Make good use of fresh rosemary in this marinade, which is ideal for barbecued salmon.

Serves 4

several sprigs of fresh rosemary

6 tbsp olive oil

3 tbsp tarragon vinegar

1 garlic clove, crushed

2 scallions, chopped

4 salmon steaks

salt and ground black pepper

lemon wedges and mixed salad
  greens, to serve

COOK'S TIP

Include other chopped fresh herbs in the marinade if you wish. Chervil, thyme, parsley, sage, oregano, and chives are all suitable. This marinade is also good with meat and poultry, including veal, pork, lamb, and chicken.

Discard any coarse stalks and damaged leaves from the rosemary, then chop the leaves very finely. Mix with the oil, vinegar, garlic, scallions, and salt and pepper.

Place the fish in a bowl and pour over the rosemary marinade. Cover and leave in a cool place for 4–6 hours.

Brush the fish with the marinade and cook under a preheated hot broiler or over a barbecue, turning occasionally, until it is tender. Baste the fish with the marinade while it cooks. Serve with lemon wedges and salad greens.

ROSEMARY MULLET IN BANANA LEAVES

The exceptionally sweet and rich flavor of red mullet is enhanced by the aroma of rosemary, and banana leaves help to seal in the juices of this firm-textured fish.

Serves 4

8 small red mullet or kingfish, about 6oz each

8 fresh rosemary sprigs, plus extra to garnish

banana leaves or wax paper

2 tbsp olive oil

salt and ground black pepper

Preheat the oven to 425°F.

Wash, scale, and clean the fish or ask your fish store to do this for you. Lay a rosemary sprig inside the cavity of each fish. Cut a piece of banana leaf or a sheet of wax paper large enough to wrap each fish.

Drizzle the mullet with a little olive oil and season well. Wrap each fish securely in the banana leaves or wax paper. Place the packets on a cookie sheet, seam side down. Bake in the oven for about 12 minutes, until cooked through and tender. Unwrap the packets to serve and garnish with more fresh rosemary sprigs.

COOK'S TIP
There are two varieties of red mullet available. The best is actually called golden mullet.

ROSEMARY BAKED FISH

This North African dish, evoking all the color and rich tastes of Mediterranean cuisine, is served with an unusual and delicious rosemary-flavored sauce.

Serves 4

1 whole white fish, about 2½lb,
   scaled and cleaned

2 tsp coriander seeds

4 garlic cloves, sliced

2 tsp chili sauce

6 tbsp olive oil

6 plum tomatoes, sliced

1 mild onion, sliced

3 preserved lemons or 1 fresh lemon

plenty of fresh herbs, such as
   rosemary, bay leaves, and thyme

salt and ground black pepper

extra fresh herbs, to garnish

For the sauce

½ cup light sesame seed paste

juice of 1 lemon

1 garlic clove, crushed

3 tbsp finely chopped fresh rosemary

Preheat the oven to 400°F. Grease the base and sides of a large, shallow ovenproof dish or roasting pan.

Slash the fish diagonally on both sides with a sharp knife. Finely crush the coriander seeds and garlic using a pestle and mortar. Mix with the chili sauce and about 4 tbsp of the olive oil.

Spread a little of the chili sauce mixture inside the cavity of the fish. Spread the remainder over each side of the fish and set aside.

Scatter the tomatoes, onion, and preserved or fresh lemon into the prepared dish or pan. (Thinly slice the lemon if using a fresh one.) Sprinkle with the remaining oil and season with salt and pepper. Lay the fish on top and tuck plenty of rosemary and other herbs around it. Bake in the oven uncovered, for about 25 minutes, or until the fish has turned opaque – test by piercing the thickest part with a knife.

Meanwhile, make the sauce. Put the sesame seed paste, lemon juice, garlic, and rosemary in a small saucepan with ½ cup water and add a little salt and pepper. Cook gently until smooth and heated through. Serve in a separate dish, alongside the baked fish.

Meat Dishes

Rosemary is the perfect herb for flavoring meat. Lamb and rosemary are an ideal marriage of flavors as the herb cuts the fattiness of the meat. Rosemary also balances the richness of pork and goes well with beef.

ROSEMARY LAMB WITH MUSTARD

Here rosemary is combined with mustard and breadcrumbs to make a crisp coating for rack of lamb.

Serves 6–8

2 or 3 garlic cloves

4oz (about 4 slices) white or whole
   wheat bread, torn into pieces

1 tbsp rosemary leaves

1½ tbsp Dijon mustard

2 tbsp olive oil

3 racks of lamb (7–8 ribs each),
   trimmed of fat, bones trimmed

ground black pepper

fresh rosemary sprigs, to garnish

boiled new potatoes, to serve

COOK'S TIP

*This recipe is perfect for
entertaining, allowing you time
with your guests. You can coat
the lamb with the crust before
they arrive and put it in the
oven to cook when you sit
down to eat the first course.*

Preheat the oven to 425°F.

In a food processor fitted with a metal blade, with the machine running, drop the garlic through the feed tube and process until finely chopped. Add the bread, rosemary, mustard, and a little pepper and process until combined, then slowly pour in the oil.

Press the mixture onto the meaty side and ends of the racks of lamb, completely covering the surface. Put the racks in a shallow roasting pan and roast for about 25 minutes for medium-rare or 3–5 minutes more for medium (a meat thermometer inserted into the thickest part of the meat should register 135–140°F for medium-rare to medium).

Transfer the meat to a carving board. Cut between the bones into chops. Serve garnished with rosemary and accompanied by boiled new potatoes.

ROSEMARY LAMB CHOP SAUTÉ

When lamb is sautéed with rosemary in a heavy pan, a delicious sauce can be made by deglazing the sediment left behind with a little wine.

Serves 4

4 lamb English or loin chops, about 6oz each

1 tbsp olive oil

3 fresh rosemary sprigs

5 tbsp red wine

scant 1 cup chicken stock

1 tsp cornstarch

1 tsp Dijon mustard

½ tsp black olive paste (optional)

2 tsp white wine vinegar

2 tbsp sweet butter

salt and ground black pepper

cooked new potatoes, carrots and petits pois, to serve

Season the lamb with pepper and moisten with oil. Heat a large, heavy-based skillet over medium heat, add the rosemary, and lay the meat over the top. Allow 6–8 minutes for medium-rare or 12–15 minutes for well-done lamb, turning once during the cooking time. Transfer to a warm plate, cover, and allow the juices to settle.

Pour any excess oil from the skillet and discard the rosemary. Return the skillet to the heat and heat the sediment until it browns. Add the wine and stir with a flat wooden spoon to loosen, scraping the base of the skillet. Pour in the chicken stock and simmer.

Combine the cornstarch, mustard, and olive paste, if using, in a small bowl, adding 1 tbsp of cold water to soften. Stir the cornstarch mixture into the skillet and simmer briefly until thickened. Add the vinegar, then stir in the butter. Arrange the potatoes, carrots, petits pois, and lamb chops on 4 plates, pour over the sauce, and serve.

LAMB WITH ROSEMARY AND MUSTARD

A rosemary and mustard marinade brings a wonderful flavor to this broiled or barbecued lamb.

Serves 6–8

4oz Dijon mustard

1–2 garlic cloves, finely chopped

2 tbsp olive oil

2 tbsp lemon juice

2 tbsp chopped fresh rosemary or

*   1 tbsp crumbled dried rosemary*

5lb leg of lamb, boned and butterflied

salt and ground black pepper

Combine the mustard, garlic, oil, lemon juice, rosemary, salt, and pepper in a shallow glass or ceramic dish. Mix well together.

Add the leg of lamb, secured with skewers, and rub the mustard mixture all over it. Cover the dish and leave the meat to marinate at room temperature for at least 3 hours.

Preheat the broiler or light the barbecue. Place the lamb flat on the rack and spread with any mustard mixture left in the dish. If broiling, set the lamb 4–5in from the heat. Cook under the broiler or over charcoal until the lamb is crusty and golden brown on the outside, 10–15 minutes on each side for rare meat, 20 minutes for medium, or 25 minutes for well-done.

Transfer the lamb to a carving board and leave to rest for at least 10 minutes before carving into neat, but quite thick slices for serving.

BEEF BRAID

The attractive braided pastry encloses a rosemary-flavored mixture of ground beef, vegetables, and cheese.

Serves 4

1 tbsp oil

4 cups ground beef

2 leeks, sliced

1 tbsp tomato paste

1 tbsp chopped fresh rosemary

2 tbsp all-purpose flour

⅔ cup beef stock

1lb prepared shortcrust pastry

flour, for dusting

2 tbsp freshly grated hard cheese

1 egg, beaten

salt and ground black pepper

sprig of fresh rosemary, to garnish

new potatoes and green beans,

   to serve

Preheat the oven to 375°F.

Heat the oil in a large pan, add the ground beef, and cook for 5 minutes. Stir in the leeks, tomato paste, and fresh rosemary. Season well to taste. Add the flour and cook for 1 minute. Stir in the stock gradually and cook for a further 20 minutes. Let the mixture cool.

Roll out the pastry on a lightly floured counter to a rectangle about 12 x 10in. Place the ground beef mixture in the center of the pastry along its length. Top with the grated cheese. Make parallel diagonal cuts either side of the filling, fold in each pastry end, and then alternate pastry strips. Brush with beaten egg and bake for 40 minutes until the pastry is golden brown. Garnish and serve with new potatoes and green beans.

ROAST LEG OF LAMB WITH ROSEMARY

Served with navy or green navy beans and rich gravy, this French-style roast is a homage to rosemary.

Serves 8–10

6–7lb leg of lamb

3 or 4 garlic cloves

olive oil

fresh or dried leaves of rosemary

1lb dried navy or green navy beans,
*   soaked overnight in cold water*

1 bay leaf

2 tbsp red wine

⅔ cup lamb or beef stock

2 tbsp butter

salt and ground black pepper

watercress, to garnish

Preheat the oven to 425°F. Wipe the leg of lamb with damp paper towels and dry the fat covering well. Cut 2 or 3 of the garlic cloves into 10–12 slivers; then, with the tip of a knife, cut 10–12 slits in the lamb and insert the garlic slivers into the slits. Rub with oil, season with salt and pepper, and sprinkle with rosemary.

Set the lamb on a rack in a shallow roasting pan and put in the oven. After 15 minutes, reduce the heat to 350°F and continue to roast for 1¾–2 hours (about 18 minutes per 1lb) or until a meat thermometer inserted into the thickest part of the meat registers 135–140°F for medium-rare to medium meat or 150°F for well-done.

Meanwhile, drain and rinse the beans and put in a saucepan with enough fresh water to cover generously. Add the remaining garlic and the bay leaf, then bring to a boil. Reduce the heat and simmer for 45 minutes–1 hour or until tender.

Transfer the roast to a board and allow to stand, loosely covered, for 10–15 minutes. Skim off the fat from the cooking juices, then add the wine and stock to the roasting pan. Boil over a medium heat, stirring and scraping the base of the pan, until slightly reduced. Strain into a warm gravy boat or pitcher.

Drain the beans, discard the bay leaf, then toss the beans with the butter until it melts. Season with salt and pepper. Transfer the lamb to a serving dish, garnish with watercress, and serve with the beans and the sauce.

Barbecued Lamb with Rosemary

A traditional mixture of parsley, sage, rosemary, and thyme – the herbs of the popular folk song – adds a really summery flavor to this simple lamb dish.

Serves 4

1 leg of lamb, about 4½ lb
1 garlic clove, thinly sliced
handful of fresh rosemary
handful of fresh flat leaf parsley
handful of fresh sage
handful of fresh thyme
6 tbsp dry sherry
4 tbsp walnut oil
1¼lb medium potatoes
salt and ground black pepper

Cook's Tip

If you have a spit-roasting attachment for your barbecue (or oven), the lamb can be rolled with herbs inside, tied securely, and spit-roasted for 1½ hours. You can cook larger pieces of lamb on the spit.

Place the lamb on a board smooth side downward, so that you can see where the bone lies. Using a sharp knife, make a long cut through the flesh down to the bone. Scrape away the meat from the bone on both sides, until the bone is completely exposed. Remove the bone and cut away any sinews and excess fat.

Cut through the thickest part of the meat to enable it to open out as flat as possible. Make several cuts in the lamb with a sharp knife, and push slivers of garlic and sprigs of herbs into them.

Place the meat in a bowl and pour over the sherry and oil. Chop the remaining herbs and scatter over the meat. Cover and leave to marinate in the refrigerator for at least 30 minutes.

Remove the lamb from the marinade and season. Place on a medium-hot barbecue and cook for 30–35 minutes, turning occasionally and basting with the reserved marinade.

Scrub the potatoes, then cut them in thick slices. Brush them with the marinade and place them around the lamb. Cook for about 15–20 minutes, turning occasionally, until they are golden brown.

ROSEMARY AND JUNIPER BEEF STEW

Marinating develops a rich base for casseroles and stews. Here, the complementary flavors of rosemary and juniper berries are dominant.

Serves 4–6

1½lb blade steak, trimmed and cut
    into 1in cubes
2 carrots, cut into sticks
8oz baby onions or shallots
4oz button mushrooms
4 fresh rosemary sprigs
8 juniper berries, lightly crushed
8 black peppercorns, lightly crushed
1¼ cups red wine
2 tbsp vegetable oil
⅔ cup stock
2 tbsp beurre manié
salt
broccoli, to serve

COOK'S TIP
*To make beurre manié,
combine equal quantities of
flour and butter.*

Place the meat in a bowl and add the carrots, onions or shallots, mushrooms, rosemary, juniper berries, and peppercorns. Pour over the wine, cover, and leave in a cool place for 4–5 hours, stirring occasionally.

Remove the meat and vegetables from the bowl with a slotted spoon and set aside. Strain the marinade into a pitcher.

Preheat the oven to 325°F. Heat the oil in a skillet and fry the meat and vegetables in batches until lightly browned. Pour over the reserved marinade and stock and bring to a boil, stirring from time to time. Transfer to a casserole, cover, and cook in the oven for 2 hours.

Twenty minutes before the end of cooking stir in the beurre manié, cover again, and return to the oven. Season to taste and serve with broccoli.

PROVENÇAL BEEF WITH ROSEMARY

Fish sauces with meat have sometimes been considered odd, but this one works extremely well and is beautifully balanced by an abundance of rosemary and garlic in the beef marinade.

Serves 4

3lb trimmed beef fillet
1 large bunch fresh rosemary
4 garlic cloves, crushed
1¼ cups olive oil
salt and ground black pepper
rosemary, to garnish
tomato wedges, to serve

For the tapenade

2oz can anchovies
1 cup pitted black olives
2 garlic cloves
2 egg yolks
⅔ cup olive oil
2 tsp lemon juice

Put the beef in a non-metallic dish and cover with the rosemary, garlic, oil, and seasoning. Leave to marinate for at least 2 hours in the refrigerator.

For the tapenade, drain the anchovies and leave them to soak in a bowl of cold water for about 20 minutes. Drain again.

In a food processor fitted with a metal blade, roughly chop the anchovies, olives, and garlic cloves. Add the egg yolks and gradually pour in the oil while the blade is still running. Stir in the lemon juice and season to taste. Chill for 30 minutes.

Preheat the oven to 375°F. Spread the tapenade over the beef and cook in the oven for 45 minutes. Serve sliced with tomato wedges, garnished with rosemary.

HONEY-ROAST PORK WITH ROSEMARY

Rosemary, thyme, and honey add flavor and sweetness to pork tenderloin, while mustard brings piquancy.

Serves 4

2 tbsp clear honey

2 tbsp Dijon mustard

1 tsp chopped fresh rosemary

½ tsp chopped fresh thyme

1lb pork tenderloin, trimmed of
   any fat

¼ tsp pink and green peppercorns,
   crushed

sprigs of fresh rosemary and thyme,
   to garnish

potato gratin and steamed
   cauliflower, to serve

For the red onion confit

4 red onions

1½ cups vegetable stock

1 tbsp red wine vinegar

1 tbsp superfine sugar

1 garlic clove, crushed

2 tbsp ruby port

pinch of salt

Preheat the oven to 350°F.

Mix together the honey, mustard, rosemary, and thyme in a small bowl. Spread the mixture over the pork and sprinkle with the peppercorns. Place in a non-stick roasting pan and cook in the oven for 35–45 minutes.

For the red onion confit, slice the onions into rings and put them into a heavy-based saucepan. Add the stock, vinegar, sugar, and garlic clove, bring to a boil, then reduce the heat. Cover and simmer for 15 minutes.

Uncover the pan, pour in the port, and continue to simmer, stirring occasionally, until the onions are soft and the juices thick and syrupy. Season to taste with salt.

Cut the pork into slices and arrange on 4 warm plates. Serve, garnished with fresh rosemary and thyme sprigs, with the red onion confit, potato gratin, and cauliflower.

MARSALA PORK WITH ROSEMARY

Usually used in desserts, here Sicilian marsala partners aromatic rosemary to flavor pork escalopes.

Serves 4

1oz dried cep or porcini mushrooms

4 pork escalopes

2 tsp balsamic vinegar

8 garlic cloves

1 tbsp butter

3 tbsp marsala

several sprigs of fresh rosemary

10 juniper berries, crushed

salt and ground black pepper

cooked noodles and green vegetables,
to serve

COOK'S TIP

Use good-quality pork escalopes that will not be submerged by the strong flavor of this unusual sauce.

Put the dried mushrooms in a bowl and just cover with hot water. Leave to stand.

Brush the pork with 1 tsp of the vinegar and season with salt and pepper. Put the garlic cloves, unpeeled, in a small pan of boiling water and cook for 10 minutes until soft. Drain and set aside.

Melt the butter in a large skillet. Add the pork and fry quickly until browned on the underside. Turn the meat over and cook for another minute.

Drain the mushrooms in a fine strainer and reserve the soaking liquid. Add the mushrooms and 4 tbsp of the reserved liquid to the pork, followed by the marsala, rosemary, garlic cloves, juniper berries, and remaining vinegar. Simmer gently for about 3 minutes until the pork is cooked through. Season lightly and serve hot with noodles and green vegetables.

Poultry Dishes

Used sparingly, rosemary adds a fresh, uplifting flavor to a variety of poultry dishes, including stir-fries, roasts, and pot-roasts. Rosemary-flavored poultry, especially chicken, is particularly tasty served cold.

CHICKEN PACKETS WITH ROSEMARY

Rosemary butter is used to moisten tender chicken and to brush the filo pastry enclosing it.

Serves 4

4 chicken breast fillets, skinned

⅝ cup butter, softened

6 tbsp chopped fresh rosemary

1 tsp lemon juice

5 large sheets filo pastry, thawed
    if frozen

1 egg, beaten

2 tbsp grated Parmesan cheese

salt and ground black pepper

Season the chicken fillets and fry in 2 tbsp of the butter to seal and brown lightly. Allow to cool.

Preheat the oven to 375°F. Put the remaining butter, the rosemary, lemon juice, and seasoning in a food processor and process until smooth. Melt half the herb butter.

Brush 1 sheet of filo pastry with herb butter. Fold it in half and brush again with butter. Place a chicken fillet about 1in from the top. Dot the chicken with a quarter of the remaining herb butter. Fold in the sides of the pastry, then roll up to enclose the filling completely. Place seam side down on a lightly greased cookie sheet. Repeat with the other chicken fillets.

Brush the filo packets with beaten egg. Cut the last sheet of filo into strips, scrunch, and arrange on top. Brush with the egg glaze, then sprinkle the packets with Parmesan. Bake in the oven for about 35–40 minutes.

COOK'S TIP

*This recipe also works well
with turkey breast fillets.*

CHICKEN LIVER STIR-FRY WITH ROSEMARY

The final sprinkling of lemon, rosemary, and garlic gives this quick, easy, and inexpensive dish a delightful fresh flavor and wonderful aroma.

Serves 4

1¼ lb chicken livers

6 tbsp butter

6oz field mushrooms

2oz chanterelle mushrooms

3 garlic cloves, finely chopped

2 shallots, finely chopped

⅔ cup medium sherry

3 fresh rosemary sprigs

rind of 1 lemon, cut into thin strips

2 tbsp chopped fresh rosemary

salt and ground black pepper

flat leaf parsley, to garnish

4 thick slices white toast, to serve

Clean and trim the chicken livers to remove any gristle or muscle. Season them generously with salt and pepper, tossing well to coat thoroughly.

Heat a wok or heavy-based skillet and add 1 tbsp of the butter. When it has melted, add the livers in batches (melting more butter where necessary but reserving 2 tbsp for the vegetables) and flash-fry until golden brown. Drain with a perforated spoon and transfer to a plate, then place in a low oven to keep warm.

Cut the field mushrooms into thick slices and cut the chanterelles in half, or leave whole, depending on their size.

Re-heat the wok or skillet and add the remaining butter. When it has melted, stir in two-thirds of the chopped garlic and the shallots and stir-fry for 1 minute until golden brown. Stir in the mushrooms and continue to cook for a further 2 minutes.

Add the sherry, bring to a boil, and simmer for 2–3 minutes until syrupy. Add 3 rosemary sprigs, salt, and pepper and return the livers to the pan. Stir-fry for 1 minute. Sprinkle with a mixture of lemon rind, chopped rosemary, and the remaining chopped garlic, garnish with flat leaf parsley, and serve with slices of toast.

CHICKEN WITH GARLIC AND ROSEMARY

A sweet wine and garlic sauce coats chicken gently scented with rosemary and thyme.

Serves 8

4½lb chicken pieces

2 tbsp olive oil

1 large onion, halved and sliced

3 large garlic bulbs, about 7oz,
*   separated into cloves and peeled*

⅔ cup dry white wine

¾ cup chicken stock

4–5 fresh rosemary sprigs

2 fresh thyme sprigs

1 bay leaf

salt and ground black pepper

COOK'S TIP
Use fresh, new season's garlic if you can find it. There's no need to peel the cloves if the skin is not papery, just remove the outer layer. In France, the cooked garlic cloves are sometimes spread on toasted country bread.

Preheat the oven to 375°F. Pat the chicken pieces dry with paper towels and season with salt and pepper.

Heat the olive oil in a large flameproof casserole and add the chicken pieces in batches, skin side down. Brown over a medium-high heat, turning frequently. Transfer the chicken to a plate

Add the onion and garlic to the casserole, cover, and cook over a medium-low heat until lightly browned, stirring frequently.

Add the wine and bring to a boil; return the chicken to the casserole. Add the stock and herbs and bring back to a boil. Cover and transfer to the oven. Cook for 25 minutes or until the chicken is tender and the juices run clear when the thickest part of the thigh is pierced with a knife.

Remove the chicken pieces from the casserole and strain the cooking liquid. Discard the herbs, transfer the onion and garlic to a food processor, and purée until smooth. Skim off any fat from the cooking liquid and discard. Return the cooking liquid to the casserole. Stir in the garlic and onion purée, return the chicken to the casserole, and reheat gently for 3–4 minutes before serving.

ROSEMARY POT-ROAST

Pot-roasting in the French manner ensures that spring chickens, which tend to be rather bland, absorb all the wonderful flavors of young vegetables and fresh rosemary.

Serves 4

1 tbsp olive oil

1 onion, sliced

1 large garlic clove, sliced

½ cup diced lightly smoked bacon

2 spring chickens, about 1¼lb each,
*   or 4 small spring chickens, about*
*   12oz each*

2 tbsp melted butter

2 baby celery hearts, each cut into 4

8 baby carrots

2 small zucchini, cut into chunks

8 small new potatoes

2½ cups chicken stock

⅔ cup dry white wine

3 fresh rosemary sprigs

1 fresh thyme sprig

1 bay leaf

1 tbsp butter, softened

1 tbsp all-purpose flour

salt and ground black pepper

fresh herbs, to garnish

Preheat the oven to 375°F. Heat the olive oil in a large flameproof casserole and add the onion, garlic, and bacon. Sauté for 5–6 minutes until the onion has softened.

Brush the chickens with a little of the melted butter and season well. Lay on top of the onion mixture and arrange the prepared vegetables around them. Pour the chicken stock and wine around the birds and add the herbs.

Cover, bake in the oven for 20 minutes, then remove the lid, and brush the birds with the remaining melted butter. Bake for a further 25–30 minutes until golden.

Transfer the spring chickens to a warm serving platter. If using larger ones, cut them in half with poultry shears or scissors. Remove the vegetables from the casserole with a perforated spoon and arrange them around the birds. Cover with foil and keep warm.

Discard the herbs from the cooking juices. In a bowl mix together the softened butter and flour to form a paste. Bring the liquid in the casserole to a boil and then whisk in teaspoonfuls of the paste until the sauce has thickened. Season the sauce and serve with the spring chickens and vegetables, garnished with fresh herbs.

ROSEMARY DUCK AND CHESTNUT SAUCE

A sauce of sweet chestnuts complements duck breast that has been steeped in a garlic and herb marinade.

Serves 4–5

several sprigs of fresh rosemary
1 garlic clove, thinly sliced
2 tbsp olive oil
4 duck breasts, boned and fat
removed

For the chestnut sauce

1lb chestnuts
1 tsp oil
1½ cups milk
1 small onion, finely chopped
1 carrot, finely chopped
1 small bay leaf
2 tbsp cream, warmed
salt and ground black pepper

COOK'S TIP
The chestnut sauce may be prepared in advance and kept in the refrigerator for up to 2 days. It can also be frozen. Thaw before reheating.

Pull the leaves from 1 rosemary sprig. Combine them with the garlic and oil in a shallow bowl. Pat the duck breasts dry with paper towels and brush with the marinade. Allow to stand for at least 2 hours before cooking.

Meanwhile make the chestnut sauce. Preheat the oven to 350°F. Cut a cross in the flat side of each chestnut with a sharp knife. Place the chestnuts in a baking pan with the oil and shake the pan until the nuts are coated well. Bake in the oven for about 20 minutes. Allow to cool slightly, then peel.

Place the peeled chestnuts in a heavy-based saucepan with the milk, onion, carrot, and bay leaf. Cook slowly for about 10–15 minutes until the chestnuts are very tender. Season with salt and pepper. Discard the bay leaf. Press the mixture through a strainer.

Preheat the broiler or prepare a barbecue. Broil the duck breasts until medium-rare, about 6–8 minutes. The meat should be pink when sliced.

Return the chestnut sauce to the saucepan. Heat gently while the duck is cooking. Just before serving, stir in the cream. If the sauce is too thick, add a little more cream.

Slice the duck breasts into rounds and arrange on warm plates. Serve with the heated sauce and garnish with the remaining rosemary sprigs.

Vegetable Dishes and Breads

The strong fragrance of rosemary brings to life all sorts of vegetarian dishes and vegetable accompaniments, especially pasta and pulses. It is excellent with mildly flavored vegetables, as well as tomatoes and bell peppers.

ROSEMARY RÖSTI

Rosemary is an excellent partner for potatoes in this tasty, traditional Swiss dish.

Serves 4

12oz par-cooked potatoes

3 tbsp olive oil

2 tsp chopped fresh rosemary

pinch of freshly grated nutmeg

3oz smoked bacon, cut into cubes

salt flakes and ground black pepper

sprigs of fresh rosemary, to garnish

4 quail eggs, to serve

COOK'S TIP

Serve this dish for a hearty and warming winter breakfast or as an unusual starter to a family meal – hungry, growing children love it.

Coarsely grate the potatoes and thoroughly pat dry on paper towels to remove all the moisture.

Heat a heavy-based skillet, then add 2 tbsp of the oil. When the oil is hot, add the potatoes and cook them in batches until crisp and golden. This will take about 10 minutes. Drain them on paper towels, mix with the rosemary, nutmeg, and plenty of seasoning, and keep warm.

Add the bacon to the hot skillet and stir-fry until crisp. Sprinkle the bacon on top of the potato.

Heat the skillet again and add the remaining oil. When the oil is hot, fry the quail eggs for about 2 minutes. Make a pile of the rosemary rösti, garnish with sprigs of fresh rosemary, and serve with the eggs.

VEGETABLE CANNELLONI WITH ROSEMARY

A subtle hint of rosemary enhances this milk-flavored pasta dish, evoking a Mediterranean mood.

Serves 4–6

1 onion, finely chopped

2 garlic cloves, crushed

2 carrots, coarsely grated

2 celery stalks, finely chopped

⅔ cup vegetable stock

4oz red or green lentils

14oz can chopped tomatoes

2 tbsp tomato paste

½ tsp ground ginger

1 tsp chopped fresh rosemary

1 tsp chopped fresh thyme

3 tbsp butter

generous 1 tbsp all-purpose flour

2½ cups milk

1 bay leaf

large pinch of grated nutmeg

16–18 cannelloni

4 tbsp grated hard cheese

4 tbsp grated Parmesan cheese

½ cup fresh white breadcrumbs

salt and ground black pepper

flat leaf parsley, to garnish

To make the filling, put the onion, garlic, carrots, and celery into a large saucepan, add half the stock, cover, and cook for 5 minutes or until the vegetables are tender.

Add the lentils, chopped tomatoes, tomato paste, ginger, rosemary, thyme, and seasoning. Bring to a boil, cover, and cook for 20 minutes. Remove the lid and cook for a further 10 minutes until thick and soft. Set aside to cool.

To make the sauce, put the butter, flour, milk, and bay leaf into a pan and whisk over the heat until thick and smooth. Season with salt, pepper, and nutmeg. Discard the bay leaf.

Fill the uncooked cannelloni by piping the filling into each tube. (It is easiest to hold them upright with one end flat on a board, while piping into the other end.)

Preheat the oven to 350°F. Spoon half the sauce into the bottom of an 8in square ovenproof dish. Lay 2 rows of filled cannelloni on top and spoon over the remaining sauce. Scatter over the cheeses and breadcrumbs. Bake in the oven for 30–40 minutes. Broil to brown the top, if necessary. Garnish with flat leaf parsley before serving.

ROSEMARY ROASTIES

These unusual roast potatoes, cooked in their skins, are given an extra lift by the addition of rosemary.

Serves 4

2lb small red potatoes

2 tsp walnut or sunflower oil

2 tbsp fresh rosemary leaves

salt and paprika

sprigs of fresh rosemary, to garnish

Preheat the oven to 475°F.

Leave the potatoes whole with the peel on; if large, cut in half. Place the potatoes in a large pan of cold water and bring to a boil. Drain them well.

Drizzle the walnut or sunflower oil over the potatoes and shake the pan to coat them evenly.

Tip the potatoes into a shallow roasting pan. Sprinkle with rosemary, salt, and paprika. Roast for 30 minutes or until crisp. Garnish and serve hot.

ROSEMARY AND GARLIC TOASTS

A delicious rosemary-flavored appetizer or accompaniment to meat or vegetarian main dishes.

Serves 4

2 whole garlic heads

extra virgin olive oil

sprigs of fresh rosemary

1 Italian loaf or thick baguette

salt and ground black pepper

Slice the tops off the heads of garlic with a sharp knife. Brush with oil, and then wrap in foil, with a few sprigs of rosemary. Cook on a medium-hot barbecue for 25–30 minutes, turning occasionally, until soft.

Slice the bread and brush generously with oil. Toast on the barbecue until golden, turning once.

Squeeze the garlic cloves from their skins onto the toasts. Chop some rosemary and sprinkle it over the toasts, together with a little extra olive oil and salt and pepper to taste.

COOK'S TIP

Roast a few slices of eggplant, bell pepper, and onion over the barbecue to spread over the toasts for variety.

ROSEMARY AND SEA-SALT FOCACCIA

Focaccia is an Italian soft, flat bread made with olive oil. Here it is given added flavor with fresh rosemary and a sprinkling of coarse sea salt.

Makes 1 loaf

3 cups all-purpose flour

½ tsp salt

2 tsp fast-rising dried yeast

about 1 cup lukewarm water

3 tbsp olive oil

1 small red onion

*leaves from 1 large fresh
    rosemary sprig*

1 tsp coarse sea salt

Sift the flour and salt into a large mixing bowl. Stir in the yeast, then make a well in the center of the dry ingredients. Pour in the water and 2 tbsp of the oil. Mix well, adding a little more water if the mixture seems dry.

Turn the dough onto a lightly floured counter and knead for about 10 minutes until smooth and elastic.

Place the dough in a greased bowl, cover, and leave in a warm place for about 1 hour until doubled in size. Punch down and knead the dough for 2–3 minutes.

Roll out the dough to a large round, about ½in thick, and transfer to a greased cookie sheet. Brush with the remaining oil.

Halve the onion and slice into thin wedges. Sprinkle the onion over the dough, with the rosemary and sea salt, pressing in lightly.

Using a finger, make deep indentations in the dough. Cover the surface with greased plastic wrap, then leave to rise in a warm place for 30 minutes.

Meanwhile, preheat the oven to 425°F. Remove the plastic wrap from the dough and bake the loaf in the oven for 25–30 minutes until golden. Serve warm.

ROSEMARY BREAD

Sliced thickly, this rosemary bread is delicious with cheese or soup for a light lunch or supper.

Makes 1 loaf

2 tsp fast-rising dried yeast

1½ cups whole wheat flour

1½ cups self-rising flour

2 tbsp butter, plus extra for greasing

¼ cup warm water (110°F)

1 cup milk (room temperature)

1 tbsp sugar

1 tbsp salt

1 tbsp sesame seeds

1 tbsp dried chopped onion

1 tbsp fresh rosemary leaves, plus
*   extra to decorate*

1 cup diced hard cheese

coarse salt, to decorate

Mix the yeast with the flours in a large mixing bowl. Melt the butter. Stir the warm water, milk, sugar, butter, salt, sesame seeds, onion, and rosemary into the flour mixture. Knead thoroughly until quite smooth.

Flatten the dough, then add the diced cheese. Quickly knead it in until it has been thoroughly incorporated.

Place the dough in a clean bowl greased with a little butter, turning it so that it becomes greased on all sides. Cover with a clean, dry cloth. Put it in a warm place and leave for about 1½ hours until the dough has risen and doubled in size.

Grease a 9 x 5in loaf pan with the remaining butter. Punch down the dough to remove some of the air, and shape it into a loaf. Put the loaf into the pan, cover with the clean cloth used earlier, and leave for about 1 hour until doubled in size once again. Preheat the oven to 375°F.

Bake the loaf in the oven for 30 minutes. During the last 5–10 minutes of baking, cover with foil to prevent it from becoming too dark. Remove from the pan and leave to cool on a wire rack. Decorate with rosemary leaves and coarse salt scattered on top.

ROSEMARY BEAN PURÉE WITH RADICCHIO

The slightly bitter flavors of radicchio and endive make a wonderful marriage with the creamy and aromatic rosemary-flavored bean purée.

Serves 4

14oz can cannellini beans

3 tbsp low-fat fromage blanc

finely grated rind of ½ large orange

juice of 1 large orange

1 tbsp finely chopped fresh rosemary

4 heads endive

2 medium radicchio

1 tbsp walnut oil

strips of orange rind, to garnish

Drain the beans, rinse, and drain again. Purée the beans in a blender or food processor with the fromage blanc, grated orange rind, orange juice, and rosemary. Set aside.

Cut the endive in half lengthwise. Cut each radicchio into 8 wedges.

Lay the endive and radicchio on a cookie sheet and brush with walnut oil. Broil for 2–3 minutes. Serve with the purée and scatter over the strips of orange rind.

COOK'S TIP

Other types of beans, such as navy, mung, and fava beans, could also be used.

ROSEMARY BAKED BELL PEPPERS

*Make sure that there is a basket of freshly baked warm bread at hand so that none of the delicious
rosemary-flavored juices from this dish are wasted.*

Serves 8

2 red bell peppers

2 yellow bell peppers

1 red onion, sliced

2 garlic cloves, halved

6 plum tomatoes, quartered

½ cup black olives

1 tsp soft light brown sugar

3 tbsp sherry

3–4 fresh rosemary sprigs

2 tbsp olive oil

salt and ground black pepper

COOK'S TIP

*You could use 4 or 5 well-
flavored beefsteak tomatoes
instead of plum tomatoes if you
prefer. In this case, cut them
into thick wedges instead of
into quarters.*

Preheat the oven to 400°F.
Seed and core the red and yellow bell peppers, then cut each into 12
strips. Place the bell peppers, onion, garlic, tomatoes, and olives in a large
roasting pan. Sprinkle over the sugar, then pour over the sherry. Season well,
cover with foil, and bake in the oven for 45 minutes.

Remove the foil from the pan and stir the mixture well. Add the
rosemary sprigs. Drizzle over the olive oil. Return the pan to the oven for a
further 30 minutes until the vegetables are tender. Serve hot.

POTATO, ROSEMARY, AND GARLIC PIZZA

New potatoes, smoked mozzarella, rosemary, and garlic make the flavor of this pizza unique.

Serves 2–3

12oz new potatoes

3 tbsp olive oil

2 garlic cloves, crushed

1 pizza base, 10–12in in diameter

1 red onion, thinly sliced

5oz smoked mozzarella
cheese, grated

2 tsp chopped fresh rosemary

salt and ground black pepper

2 tbsp freshly grated Parmesan
cheese, to garnish

Preheat the oven to 425°F. Cook the potatoes in boiling salted water for 5 minutes. Drain well. When cool, peel and slice thinly.

Heat 2 tbsp of the oil in a skillet. Add the sliced potatoes and garlic and fry for 5–8 minutes until the potatoes are tender.

Brush the pizza base with the remaining oil. Scatter over the onion, then arrange the potatoes on top. Sprinkle with the mozzarella and rosemary. Grind over plenty of black pepper and bake in the oven for 15–20 minutes until crisp and golden. Remove from the oven and sprinkle with the Parmesan before serving.

Vinegars, Preserves, and Drinks

Used with discretion, rosemary adds an unusual and delicious aroma, as well as a distinctive flavor, to condiments that will enhance salad dressings, roasts, and vegetables.

ROSEMARY VINEGAR

This easy-to-make rosemary-flavored vinegar will turn an ordinary salad dressing into something special.
It also makes an attractive and welcome, home-made present for gourmet friends.

Makes about 2½ cups
sprigs of fresh rosemary to fill a
2½ cup measure, plus extra
to decorate
2½ cups white distilled vinegar

COOK'S TIP
You could also use white wine
or cider vinegar instead of
distilled vinegar.

Fill a sterilized, wide-necked bottle or jar with the sprigs of rosemary. Fill to the top with vinegar. Cover tightly and place in a sunny position for 4–6 weeks.

Filter the vinegar mixture through a coffee filter paper. Discard the rosemary. Heat the vinegar until it begins to simmer, but do not boil.

Wash the bottle or jar and its lid well in hot, soapy water, rinse thoroughly, and dry in a warm oven. Pour the vinegar back into it or into other sterilized, decorative bottles. You can add a fresh sprig or two of rosemary for decorative purposes if you wish, then seal, and label. Store in a dark place. Use within 1 year.

MARINATED OLIVES WITH ROSEMARY

The addition of rosemary enlivens these scrumptious marinated olives, which make irresistible nibbles for serving with pre-dinner drinks.

Serves 4

1⅓ cups unpitted green olives

3 garlic cloves

1 tsp coriander seeds

2 small red chilies

2–3 thick lemon slices, cut into pieces

1 large fresh rosemary sprig

5 tbsp white wine vinegar

Spread out the olives and garlic on a chopping board. Using a rolling pin, crack and flatten them slightly. Crack the coriander seeds in a mortar with a pestle.

Mix the olives, garlic, coriander seeds, chilies, lemon pieces, rosemary sprig, and wine vinegar in a large bowl. Toss well, then transfer the mixture to a clean glass jar. Pour in water to cover. Store in the refrigerator for at least 5 days (preferably 10 days) before serving. Serve at room temperature.

COOK'S TIP

For a change, use a mix of caraway and cumin seeds in place of the coriander and mix black and green olives.

HERBAL PUNCH

A good party drink with more than a hint of rosemary that will have people coming back for more, this punch is a delightful non-alcoholic choice for drivers.

Serves 30 plus

2 cups clear honey

17 cups water

2 cups freshly squeezed lemon juice

3 tbsp fresh rosemary leaves, plus
    extra to decorate

8 cups sliced strawberries

2 cups freshly squeezed lime juice

8 cups sparkling mineral water

ice cubes

3–4 scented geranium or strawberry
    leaves, to decorate

Combine the honey, 4¼ cups water, one-eighth of the lemon juice, and the rosemary leaves in a saucepan. Bring to a boil, stirring until all the honey is dissolved. Remove from the heat and allow to stand for about 5 minutes. Strain into a large punch bowl.

Press the strawberries through a fine strainer into the punch bowl, add the rest of the water and lemon juice, and the lime juice, and sparkling mineral water. Stir gently. Add the ice cubes minutes before serving and float the geranium or strawberry leaves and extra rosemary leaves on the surface.

YOGURT CHEESE WITH ROSEMARY

These little spheres of cheese flavored with rosemary, thyme, and chili are bottled in olive oil.

Makes about 2lb

1¾lb Greek sheep's yogurt

½ tsp salt

2 tsp crushed dried chilies or chili
    powder

1 tbsp chopped fresh rosemary

1 tbsp chopped fresh thyme
    or oregano

1¼ cups olive oil, preferably
    garlic-flavored

Sterilize a 12in square of cheesecloth by steeping it in boiling water. Drain and lay over a large plate. Mix the yogurt with the salt and tip onto the centre of the muslin. Bring up the sides of the muslin and tie firmly with string.

Hang the bag on a kitchen cupboard handle or in a suitable position where it can be suspended with a bowl underneath to catch the whey. Leave for 2–3 days until the yogurt stops dripping.

Sterilize 2 x 1lb Mason jars or jelly jars by heating them in the oven at 300°F for 15 minutes.

Mix together the chili and herbs. Take teaspoonfuls of the cheese and roll into balls with your hands. Lower into the jars, sprinkling each layer with the herb mixture. Pour the oil over the cheese until completely covered. Store in the refrigerator for up to 3 weeks.

To serve the cheese, spoon out of the jars with a little of the flavored olive oil and spread onto lightly toasted bread.

COOK'S TIP

If your kitchen is particularly warm, find a cooler place to suspend the cheese. Alternatively, drain the cheese in the refrigerator, suspending the bag from one of the shelves and with a bowl underneath.

BELL PEPPER AND ROSEMARY JELLY

Whole sprigs of fresh rosemary are suspended in this wonderful amber-colored jelly.

Makes 4lb

1lb tomatoes, chopped

4 red bell peppers, seeded
  and chopped

2 red chilies, seeded and chopped

sprigs of fresh rosemary

1¼ cups water

1¼ cups red wine vinegar

½ tsp salt

4½ cups preserving sugar with
  added pectin

1 cup liquid pectin

Place the tomatoes, bell peppers, chilies, a few rosemary sprigs, and the water in a stainless-steel saucepan and bring to a boil. Cover and simmer for 1 hour or until the bell peppers are tender and pulpy.

Suspend a jelly bag and place a bowl underneath. Sterilize the jelly bag by pouring through boiling water. Discard the water and replace the bowl.

Pour the contents of the saucepan slowly into the jelly bag. Allow the juices to drip through slowly for several hours, but do not squeeze the bag or the jelly will become cloudy. Sterilize the jars and lids required.

Place the juice in a clean saucepan with the vinegar, salt, and sugar. Discard the pulp in the jelly bag. Heat the juice gently, stirring occasionally, until the sugar has dissolved. Boil rapidly for 3 minutes.

Remove the saucepan from the heat and stir in the liquid pectin. Skim the surface with a paper towel to remove any foam.

Pour the liquid into the sterilized jars and add a sprig of rosemary to each jar. Place a waxed disc on the surface of each and seal with a lid of cellophane paper and an elastic band. Allow to cool, then label, and decorate with ribbons. Store in a cool place.

INDEX

Barbecued lamb with rosemary, 26

Beans: rosemary bean purée with radicchio, 52

Beef: beef braid 23
 Provençal beef with rosemary, 29
 rosemary and juniper beef stew, 28

Bell pepper and rosemary jelly, 62

Bell peppers: and rosemary jelly, 62
 rosemary baked bell peppers, 53

Bread: rosemary and garlic toasts, 47
 rosemary and sea-salt focaccia, 48
 rosemary bread, 50

Cannelloni: vegetable cannelloni with rosemary, 44

Cheese: yogurt cheese with rosemary, 60

Chestnuts: rosemary duck and chestnut sauce, 40

Chicken liver stir-fry with rosemary, 34

Chicken packets with rosemary, 33

Chicken with garlic and rosemary, 36

Duck: rosemary duck and chestnut sauce, 40

Fish, rosemary baked, 16

Focaccia, rosemary and sea-salt, 48

Herbal punch, 59

Honey-roast pork with rosemary, 30

Jelly, bell pepper and rosemary, 62

Lamb: barbecued lamb with rosemary, 26
 lamb with rosemary and mustard, 22
 roast leg with rosemary, 24
 rosemary lamb chop sauté, 20
 rosemary lamb with mustard, 19

Marinated olives with rosemary, 58

Marsala pork with rosemary, 31

Olives: marinated with rosemary, 58
 Provençal beef with rosemary, 29

Pies: beef braid 23
 chicken packets with rosemary, 33

Pizza: potato, rosemary, and garlic, 54

Pork: honey-roast pork with rosemary, 30
 marsala pork with rosemary, 31

Potatoes: potato, rosemary, and garlic pizza, 54
 rosemary roasties, 46
 rosemary rösti, 43

Provençal beef with rosemary, 29

Punch, herbal, 59

Radicchio: rosemary bean purée with radicchio, 52

Red mullet: rosemary mullet in banana leaves, 14

Roast leg of lamb with rosemary, 24

Rosemary and garlic toasts, 47

Rosemary and juniper beef stew, 28

Rosemary and sea-salt focaccia, 48

Rosemary baked bell peppers, 53

Rosemary baked fish, 16

Rosemary bean purée with radicchio, 52

Rosemary bread, 50

Rosemary duck and chestnut sauce, 40

Rosemary lamb chop sauté, 20

Rosemary lamb with mustard, 19

Rosemary mullet in banana leaves, 14

Rosemary pot-roast, 38

Rosemary roasties, 46

Rosemary rösti, 43

Rosemary shortbread, 11

Rosemary vinegar, 57

Salmon with rosemary marinade, 13

Spring chicken: rosemary pot-roast, 38

Toasts, rosemary and garlic, 47

Vegetable cannelloni with rosemary, 44

Vinegar, rosemary, 57

Yogurt cheese with rosemary, 60